WAYS INTO GEOGRAPHY

Living on an Island

Louise Spilsbury

W

FRANKLIN WATTS

LONDON·SYDNEY

This edition 2012

First published in 2009 by
Franklin Watts
338 Euston Road
London NW1 3BH

Franklin Watts Australia
Level 17/207 Kent Street
Sydney NSW 2000

Series editor: Julia Bird
Art director: Jonathan Hair
Design: Shobha Mucha
Consultant: Sam Woodhouse, Associate Consultant for
Geography & Citizenship, Somerset

Picture credits:
Alamy: 7: © David Robertson; 14: (t) © Scottish Viewpoint; (b) ©Janine Wiedel Photolibrary; 16: (t)
© Pete Hill; (b) © Paul Glendell; 17: (b) © Studio9; 18: (b) © Paul Glendell. Corbis: p.6: (t) © Jason Hawkes;
10 (t): © Jason Hawkes. Getty Images: 25: © Stephen Munday. istockphoto: p.6: (b) © Ai-Lan Lee; 8:
© David Joyner; 26: (b) © istockphoto. Photographers Direct: 10: (b) © Nik Taylor; 17: (t) ©
Andrew Johnstone; 18: (m) Paul Glendell. Paul Bricknell: 9. Shutterstock: 7: © flavijus; 11: © Stephen Finn;
15: © Daniel Gale; 18: (t) © Justyna Furmanczyk; 26: (t) © Ben Heys; 27: © Huabing;
The Francis Frith Collection: p.24.

Every attempt has been made to clear copyright.
Should there be any inadvertent omission, please apply to
the publisher for rectification.

ISBN 978 1 4451 0956 5

Dewey classification: 910.91'42

A CIP catalogue record for this book is available
from the British Library.

Printed in China

Franklin Watts is a division of Hachette Children's Books,
an Hachette UK company.
www.hachette.co.uk

contents

What is an island?

An island is a piece of land that is surrounded by water.

Some islands are so small that few or no people live there.

Have you ever been on a small island?

Other islands are big. Many people live on them.

The island of Great Britain contains
Scotland, England and Wales.

Can you point
to where you
live? Can you
see any other
islands on
the map?

How do islands form? Turn the page to find out.

How islands form

Some islands are pieces of land that have become separated from the mainland by sea.

This is St Michael's Mount. When the tide is in, this becomes an island.

Kalem wants to see how islands form.
He shapes land and hills out of Plasticine.
Then he pours water in to form a sea.

Can you see how the islands form?
The sea has separated the hills from one
another to make islands. Underneath the
water, they are still joined up.

Getting to an island

Some islands are joined to the mainland by big bridges.

To get to many islands, people have to travel by ferry, helicopter, or plane.

People living on islands cannot grow
or make all the things they need.

Lorries travel on ferries to bring goods like
tinned food from the mainland.
Can you think what else people living
on an island might need?

On an island

This village is on a small island called Islay off the coast of Scotland.

Which features are natural and which were made by people?

Amy's class makes a list of the features that are natural and those that were made by people.

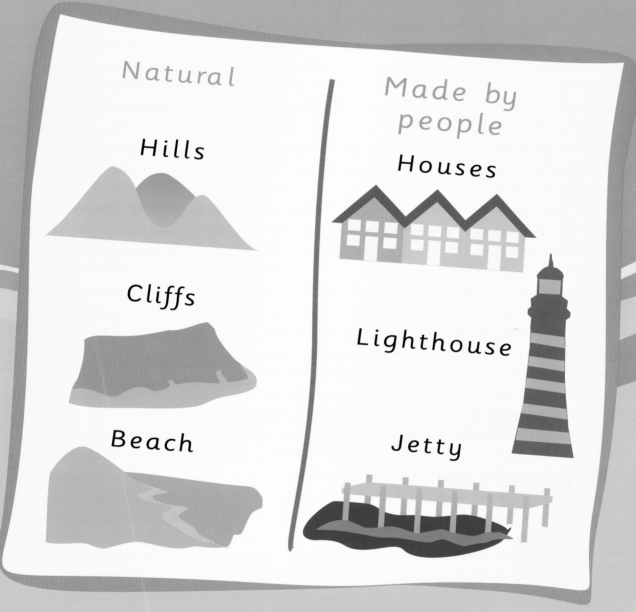

Natural
Hills
Cliffs
Beach

Made by people
Houses
Lighthouse
Jetty

How is this island home the same or different to where you live?

Island people

Small islands have only a small number of people living there.

This island has only one school. It has 12 pupils and one teacher.

How do you think it is different to your school?

The children on this island play in a playground or on the beach. There is no cinema or swimming pool here.

What would you like or dislike about living on a small island? What would you miss about your local area?

What jobs do people do on a small island? Turn the page to find out.

Island life

Some jobs on an island are the same as in a town on the mainland.

Some people work in shops, for example.

Some jobs are different. This coastguard watches out for boats from a cliff.

This island has lots of shellfish. These workers are collecting crabs to sell to other places.

This island is warmer than the mainland so daffodils grow early here. Farmers send them to the mainland by post or ship.

What jobs do people do in your local area?

Island activities

Lots of people like to visit small islands for a holiday.

These are some of the activities visitors can do on an island.

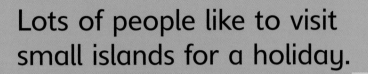

Horse-riding

Hiking

Canoeing

What other things could you do on an island holiday?

Rasheed's class makes a bar chart showing what the children in his class would like to do on an island holiday.

	Canoeing	Playing on the beach	Horse riding	Walking
12				
11				
10				
9				
8				
7				
6				
5				
4				
3				
2				
1				

What would most children like to do?
What would you like to do?

Island maps

Amy drew this map of a village on the shore of an imaginary island.

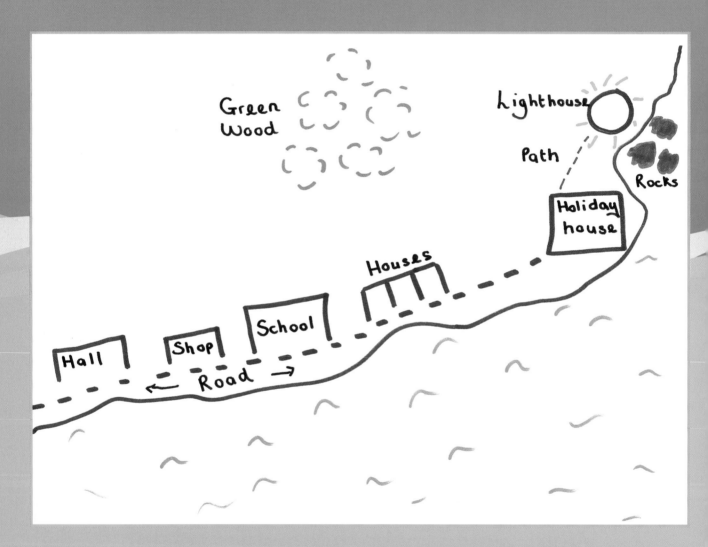

How would you describe the route from the shop to the lighthouse?

Amy makes a chart to compare the imaginary island to her real home town. What is the same and what is different?

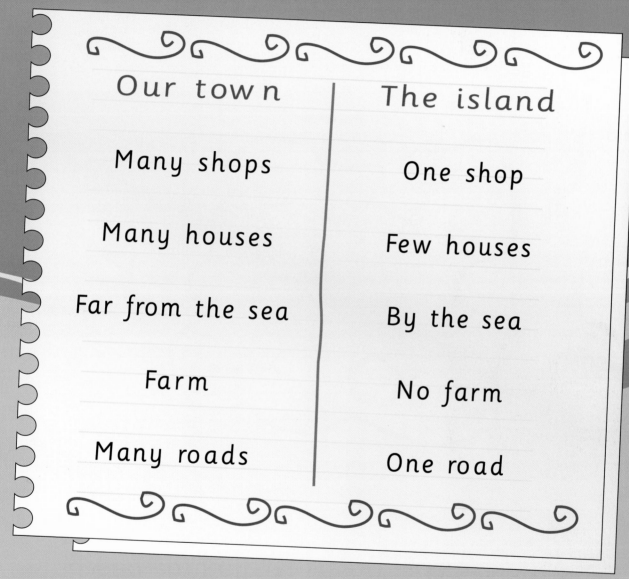

Our town	The island
Many shops	One shop
Many houses	Few houses
Far from the sea	By the sea
Farm	No farm
Many roads	One road

How is Amy's island the same or different to where you live?

What kind of imaginary island would you draw?

Treasure island

This is Rasheed's drawing of an imaginary island.

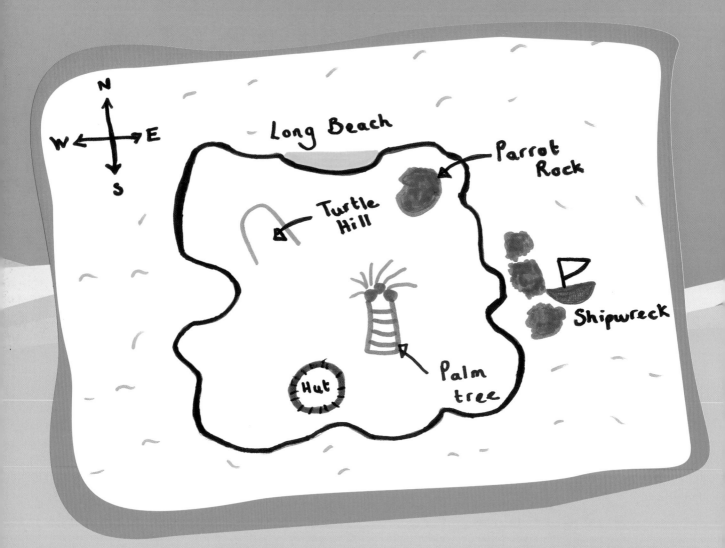

The compass points tell you the beach is on the north of the island.

What feature is on the south of the island?

Rasheed imagines pirates have buried treasure on the island. He uses a grid to remember exactly where the treasure is.

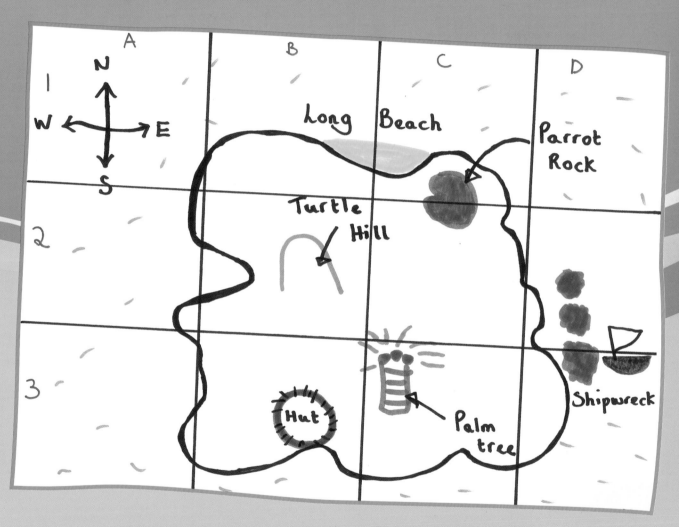

The treasure is buried in square C, 3.
What is the feature at this point on the map?

Then and now

This is a street on the Isle of Wight
50 years ago.

Visitors to the island enjoyed the peace
and quiet here then.

Today, around one million visitors come to the Isle of Wight each year. Many people come to see the famous sailing boat races.

How do you think the island has changed since the first picture was taken?

Islands of the world

On the island of Sri Lanka the weather is hot. People here earn a living by catching fish. What are the houses like?

This island in Antarctica is freezing cold. Only animals such as penguins live here.

Can you see the islands of Sri Lanka
and Antarctica marked on this map?

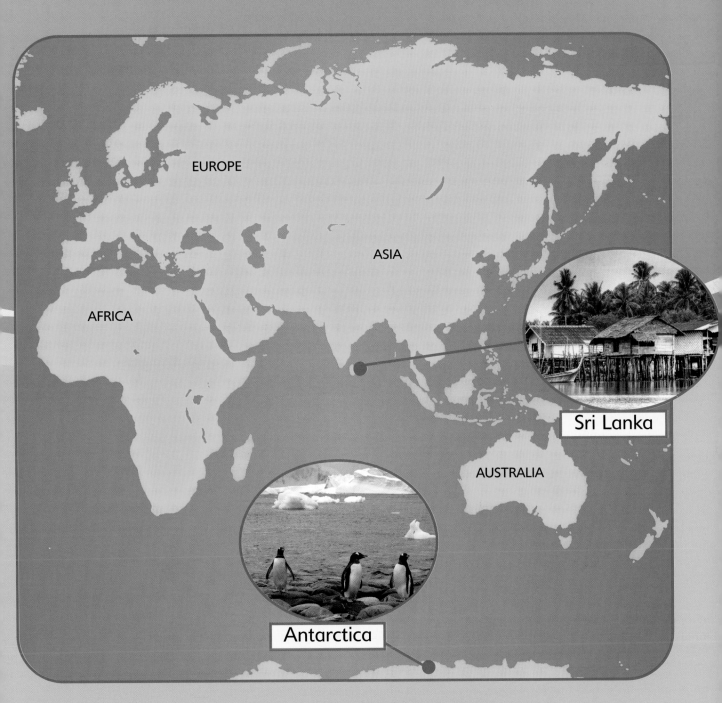

EUROPE

ASIA

AFRICA

Sri Lanka

AUSTRALIA

Antarctica

Look again at the shape of Great Britain on
page 7. Can you find Great Britain on this map?

Useful words

Bar chart – a chart that uses bars of different lengths to measure and compare amounts.

Coastguard – a person who works at the seaside. Coastguards check ships and boats are safe and make sure people obey the law at sea, for example by going at the correct speed.

Compass – a device that always points north. Compass points show us where the directions north, south, east and west are.

Features – objects on a landscape or on a map. Some features are natural, such as hills. Other features are made by people, such as houses or lighthouses.

Ferry – a boat that carries people and vehicles across water.

Goods – things people buy and sell that can be made or grown, such as clothes and food.

Grid – a pattern of lines on a map. Lines going across are usually labelled with numbers and the lines going up and down are usually labelled with letters. You can find a particular spot on a map by giving the letter and number where you find it.

Lighthouse – a tower with lights at the top that shine at night. The lights warn ships of dangerous rocks.

Mainland – a country's main area of land. The mainland is bigger than the islands near it.

Map – a drawing of a place that shows where things are. Maps usually show what a place looks like from above.

Some answers

Here are some answers to the questions we have asked in this book. Don't worry if you had different answers to ours; you may be right, too. Talk through your answers with other people and see if you can explain why they are right.

Page 11: Other goods that people on an island might need would include TV sets and computers, and other electrical appliances. They might also need books, newspapers and magazines, furniture, cars and bikes and many other goods that could not be made or grown on the island itself.

Page 18: Other things you could do on an island holiday include swimming, sailing and playing on the beach.

Page 19: The tally chart shows that most children in Rasheed's class would like to play at the beach.

Page 20: Turn left out of the shop and walk down the main road, past the school and houses. At the holiday house, turn left on to the path and walk along till you reach the lighthouse.

Page 22: The hut is the feature on the south of the island.

Page 23: The palm tree is the feature at the grid square C, 3. The treasure is buried under the palm tree!

Page 25: The modern picture suggests the island is much busier. There are more people, more traffic and the sea is full of sailing boats.

Page 26: The houses in the picture are on stilts to hold them above the water when the tide comes in.

Index

About this book

Ways into Geography is designed to encourage children to think about the local and wider world in a geographical way. This title, **Living on an island**, is a way in to study a particular kind of place, one which for most children will be a contrasting area.

By working through the book, they will also be learning the following **geographical skills**:
1. To identify and describe what places are like (National Curriculum 3a).
2. To identify and describe where places are (National Curriculum 3b).
3. To recognise how places have become the way they are (National Curriculum 3c) and to recognise how places compare with other places (National Curriculum 3d).
4. To make observations about where things are located, and to recognise changes in physical and human features (National Curriculum 4a and b).
5. To recognise changes in the environment (National Curriculum 5a).

Previous work and extension activities

It will help to have done some previous work with the children on using simple maps. On page 7, the children may need help locating the area where they live on a map, though many should have at least a rough idea. Reiterate that even though Great Britain is so big it is still an island because it is surrounded by water. Children could try making islands like the one on page 9 themselves to help them understand that islands may be joined to the mainland, but low-lying land is underwater so we cannot see it. As an extension activity, you could look at how volcanic islands form from volcanoes that erupt underneath the sea.

Following on from page 10–11, children could imagine they are stranded on an island and come up with a list of what supplies they would need most. This would help them think about what supplies a small island might need. Can they divide their list into things they really need (necessities) and things they would like to have?

To extend the activities on page 18–19, children could do their own class survey to find out which island activities their class would like to do. They could present their findings in an alternative way, such as a tally chart or pie chart.

'Treasure island' (pages 22–23) is an extension activity and children may need some help with coordinates, but the theme of pirates and buried treasure is a popular one and might inspire children to draw their own imaginary island map. You could draw a treasure map and ask them to guess where the treasure is by calling out grid coordinates for them to check.